Musings from a Jonesborough Porch

Written by Helen Thatcher

Illustrated by Ginny Wall

Jan-Carol Publishing, Inc

"every story needs a book"

Musings from a Jonesborough Porch
Written by Helen Thatcher
Illustrated by Ginny Wall

Published September 2016
Little Creek Books
Imprint of Jan-Carol Publishing, Inc
All rights reserved
Copyright © 2016 by Helen Thatcher

ISBN: 978-1-945619-06-9

You may contact the publisher:
Jan-Carol Publishing, Inc
PO Box 701
Johnson City, TN 37605
publisher@jancarolpublishing.com
jancarolpublishing.com

For Lyn, Chris and Sam,
Who have shared and loved the porch.
And for my much-loved parents.

Author's Note

A screened porch must be counted as one of the most civilized and comfortable places on which to spend a restful hour, or two. At all times affording a calm ambience from which to watch, or contemplate ideas, scenes and experiences. From sunrise to the quiet approach of night, this corner of solitude and peace is a treasure for which myself and those who have shared it are truly grateful.

Acknowledgements

My many thanks to Ginny Wall for her kindness in creating the illustrations for each essay.

The Apple

*L*ast evening, while out looking for our last cat to come home for the dark hours, the perfect apple caught my eye.

We have several apple trees which bear some fruit each year, but we don't "farm" them, so our harvests are haphazard.

As we use no "killers" for bugs, worms, June beetles, etc., we rarely find an untouched apple. If they fall they are set upon immediately by myriads of ants and later by wasps. Even while still on the tree there are "things" which begin to deface them before they are ready to be picked.

However, last evening, just at the time when the sun is deciding to go to bed after a long day's shining, approaching the apple tree and calling for our cat, there was the apple.

It hung half way down a branch and was alone, not clustered as are so many. It had a perfect skin, untouched by the pox caused by ravaging insects. Its colour was the palest yellow with a glow of red, as if wearing a touch of rouge, or faintly blushing.

It was beautiful, hanging by its stalk amidst apple leaves, basking in the rays of a tired sun as he ended his day in the western sky.

Perfect size. Perfect shape. Perfect.

Yet on the same tree, enjoying the same circumstances as its fellow apples, some already fallen to their fate with the ants, some being pecked by birds, it was the chosen apple. The one to let us see how well they can be when left alone to mature.

Maybe even in an apple tree "location" means something!

The Pond

Our pond, circular in shape, has many goldfish of varying age and size. We put in only a dozen and know we almost immediately lost two. These others have settled, met a loved-one, had babies. Now several generations share our pond and call it home.

This circular world is also home to numerous water plants—bull rushes, a forget-me-not that likes to be wet, parrot feather and others whose names are not known to us.

The most spectacular plants, however, are the water lilies and the lotus. This does not mean we favour them over the others. It simply means that they are the most showy, with bigger, brighter, more colourful blooms than some of the other, less extroverted plants. All work together to make our pond beautiful for us to look at and as a comfortable home for the fish.

It is also home to some frogs. These we see only in glimpses, but we hear them! They enjoy a kind of watery barber-shop ballad get-together of an evening, sometimes going on into the wee hours. As with many amateur groups, enthusiasm outweighs talent. Let us just say that they pose no threat to any singer! We worried that they might be ill, perhaps have some pain-causing debility, but on reflection we have decided that they simply can't sing! They are tone-deaf! They show no musical talent whatsoever!

Having said that, there is a kind of attraction in their efforts. We are pleased they have joined our pond-world, adding some more diversity to the garden and are glad they feel happy enough to sing about it.

The Lotus

The lotus is almost gone for this year. The beautiful, huge leaves remain, some yet green and bright, but others now yellowing, with others already being turned to beige—dry and shriveled.

The remains of the flower heads, too, are almost gone. Bowing their completely brown, dry seed-heads towards the water, allowing the seeds to drop there, where they may create a new plant, a new life next year.

It is fascinating to watch such a life-cycle. The growth, the energy, the strength. The bud slowly developing until the day, when all is perfect and the petals open in their freshest pink and white. Shy, they remain open only for a few hours, their early life showing beauty, promise, but also a reticence and wariness of this new-found attractiveness.

Several days and confidence allows longer blooming, a wider spread of petals to soak up the sun's rays, to expose the developing seed-head.

Then, one day the petals open fully and begin to drop—one—two—three. There is no closing around the seed-head that night. The delicate petals lie strewn on the water, floating like small boats at anchor and the seed-head is exposed, alone to face the elements.

And so it does. It holds its head allowing the seeds to see the sky, to allow them their "time in the sun."

Soon it can do it no longer and has to bow its head: a job well-done, as the seeds fall into the receptive "ground" of the water below.

Maples

*I*n our garden are many trees all loved and enjoyed for themselves, for the distinctive personality of each.

The maples are the oldest and tallest, providing wonderful summer shade, while allowing some of the sun's rays to creep through to light up different spots on its day's journey. To highlight an area of bark, a grouping of plants, a seat, a sleeping cat.

In autumn, maple colours are radiant, often set against a clear, blue sky. It is almost as if they are promising that by following their ancient cycle they will return in a wonderful new spring outfit.

As the leaves fall they are collected to add to the compost pile, so even after all their shade-giving qualities, they continue to be of use at their demise.

Winter allows the true shapes of the trees to be seen. The tracery of their branches and twigs against a winter sky; on a frosty, moonlit night when bark and branches are touched with silver and the moon herself seems to linger for a while, entangled in the branches, before moving on her night-time journey.

Our maples are home to many squirrels, whose dreys only become visible in winter, perched precariously high in the uppermost branches.

Birds perch, hide in them and sing from them. Butterflies flutter to the highest reaches before disappearing into the foliage. At night the tops are aglow with fire-fly lanterns.

We know, too, that they are home to many others, unseen by us, but known to woodpeckers, tree-creepers and wrens.

The Chestnut Tree

*O*urs is not the American chestnut, but is very pretty and has a similar spreading habit. It would be a better tree if out in a meadow, where its various "shedding" habits did not impinge on a garden. However, it is here and we love it as a growing, beautiful part of Nature.

It starts in spring with the wonderful "tails" which bring a particular fragrance to the surrounds. It is a sweet-type of smell, but not one to be captured for scent. One to be whiffed in passing only! Sadly, these pretty white tails turn brown, dropping everywhere and are not conducive to composting. Later in the year, as the leaves fall, the same applies. They are too leathery to decompose quickly.

The chestnuts themselves are beautiful. Shiny, polished brown and perfect, but sadly, usually inhabited by worms. There is a moral in this, we are sure! Before being aware of this, they were collected and laid out on a table. It was then we could hear the munching. Truly, unabashed munching!

Of course, before bursting open to reveal the nut, we have the casing. Only squirrels seem to be able to tolerate the prickles. Even as young, green coats they are vicious and do not lose their sharpness as they grow old and turn brown, lying in wait for the gardeners hand—even into the following spring!

It is not the friendliest of trees in the garden and tries the patience, but it is a tree and is loved as such and as a provider for many of our visiting and resident garden creatures.

Mouse and Man

For some reason a memory came to mind today, unconnected to anything. It is a morning and evening in Washington, D.C. Coffee is being taken at a small cafe within our hotel. For early morning there seems to be an extra "buzz" to the area, even for a big city. "Official"-looking people are hovering, in their official-looking suits and coats, with their official expressions firmly fixed to their faces. Serious, non-smiling, clean-cut. Having watched too many gangster films, it crosses the mind that this may be a "raid" of some sort. Then, as quickly, this thought is dismissed as one looks around at the clientele.

Then all is explained.

The arrival of a prominent politician, who is escorted into the hotel, taken to a private lift and disappears with his serious young men and women in their "official" outfits.

In the evening, waiting at a crossing to go to a restaurant, there is suddenly—a mouse! Town, or country mouse? Lost, or, "I know where I'm going" mouse? It joins us at the crossing, then threads its way to a grouping of large plant-pots close to a building. No fuss. No entourage. No official escort. Yet so small, so very vulnerable to so much of our world. The contrast between our morning and evening experiences was thought-provoking.

We hoped it was a town mouse and was home safely.

Carnage on Roads

The carnage on our roads has always been distressing, but now it seems worse. This may be due to many reasons, but mostly, I think, it is because few people care anymore.

In past times these wee bodies were collected. This does not mean a "proper" burial would take place, but they were removed while something of them remained. This compassion rarely exists now. Even domestic animals are left with no one who cares to weep over their demise. It is sometimes too dangerous to stop and pick-up such a corpse, that is understood, although my husband and I have done so on occasions when it was possible.

I believe in the spirit, the soul of a being, so understand that what is left is but a shell, the husk of that being. However, we make such a fuss over the husks of our own species, it would seem we could extend it to those killed by us.

Nature deals with all her dead, but cannot always cope readily with the deaths on our roads. At least she does her best, but this is not the point. We kill creatures—many, many creatures—and we don't care enough to extend them, at the very least, the dignity of decomposing in private. We see a raccoon, a possum, a cat, a dog, a squirrel, a groundhog, a rabbit, a deer—and so the list goes on. We recognize them, their wee ears still perked, often looking directly at us as we pass their inert bodies.

Then we see them—and see them—becoming less of themselves, until there only remains a dull mark on the road surface. We need to be more cognizant of the fact that this was a living being, a member of a family, a community who grieve the loss. And we need to be more caring of that loss, too.

The Storm

*T*he storm has passed, bringing wonderful rain and cooler temperatures in its wake.

Some of the thunder boomed right overhead, making us jump and the cats leap from their resting-places. No matter how settled and sound asleep they seem, they are ready in a split second to move—quickly, with great agility and elegance, as if having planned and practised for this event. Even Eilidh, our airedale, decided the better part of valour was to move to a place further from the door.

"The calm before the storm" is often used and is true, but the calm after the storm is also worth noting and appreciating. After all the flashings and boomings, the crashings and poundings, there descends a quiet, a stillness. The ground is refreshed, there are beautiful raindrops on everything, adding sparkle to wherever they cling. The branches and grasses seem inordinately stiff, where only minutes before they were performing the wildest of dances—twisting, twirling and bending in all directions. They are, once more, the calm, reasoned, sensible beings we know, conserving their energy for the next mad romp with the wind and rain.

Birds are returned to the feeders, butterflies are sipping at the flowers, bees are making their erratic way to somewhere. The garden enjoys its drink, the birdbaths are filled and even the fish seem happy to have had this infusion of rain water, coming out from under the lily pads, now that all is calm.

Derided Plants

*I*t has become the fashion, these last few years, to disdain certain plants. Said plants have become "common," victims of their own success. These poor creatures—abandoned, maligned, dismissed without ceremony.

We are not of the above number.

There are certain plants we do not like as well as others, but it is not because they are commonly-used. Many of this group have become such because they are easy to grow, have few problems, survive a variety of weathers and so we plant the ones we enjoy, much-used, or not.

Looking around the pots in our garden, we see many with "wave" petunias and busy lizzies (impatiens). It is hardly possible to be more over-used than these, except, perhaps, for the geranium—also in pots in our garden. It is sad to deride such enthusiastic growers. Bought at relatively low cost, potted and left alone, apart from some water, they grow and grow and bloom and bloom.

It seems they are rarely accosted by insects, viruses or fungi. Their sole purpose being to bloom in many colours, brighten a dark spot, overflow a sunny window-box and all for minimal care. It seems a strange quirk of human nature to ignore such an admirable invention—something pretty, colourful, long-blooming that asks for no special attention.

They give a lot for very little and we do admire them and compliment them often.

Tree Choppers

*W*e live in an area where power lines are not underground. It is ridiculous in the extreme. Overhead power lines have problems in every season. If not with animals, with cold, with limbs of trees falling on them etc. In a young, wealthy country it seems absurd that this antiquated system continues.

The reason for this coming to mind (again!) was because, this week, we have had to suffer the tree-choppers. These misguided souls, who are only doing as they have been instructed, arrive in their huge trucks, with chain saws and chopper at the ready. The sound of these is almost more than a heart can bear, as we watch to see which is next in line.

Healthy trees are distorted, some are permanently damaged, but the carnage goes on season after season. We pay no attention to the hurt we do—to the tree, obviously, but also to the life the tree supports, the shade it gives, the part it plays in keeping our climate stable. It is a sad reflection on the human race that we consider everything is here solely for our use, or disposal. With the tools we have nowadays and the rate of development, it doesn't take long to make a desert. Change completely the topography of an area. Try finding a shade tree in a parking lot!

It would be a good thing if we, supposedly intelligent beings, were to stop and think *Is there a better way?* Could we not try to work with and around the flora and fauna of our world, instead of just destroying it all? A humorous person once said that developers go into an area, chop down all the trees, then name the streets after them! True!

We need to begin thinking about more than just ourselves, be conscious of the wide array of trees, plants and animals that go to make up the wonderful tapestry that is our world. Each has a part to play. Let's not wait until they are gone before realizing how important they were.

The Attic Painting

*W*hen we came to this house it had already been "altered." The problem with altering is that not everyone is in accord with how it is done. Our home had seen many owners since its conception, so was quite severely changed.

We were, therefore, delighted to find any small remnants of the past, whatever they might be. Modernisation had taken place, some quite disastrous, but there remained a couple of "hidden treasures." Not monetary treasures, but those of interest and fascination.

In the attic, full of coal dust, was found a shoe, covered in the black dust and dried to a crisp. Abandoned, alone. Whose shoe? Why only one left? The life lived by the one who wore it? The small size and style indicated it had belonged to a woman, or girl. However, it was not going to reveal any more to us of how it lived its life when a supple, young shoe.

Then further in the attic, there was a portrait. On canvas, unframed.

A painting of a young man, elegant, soulful, looking out to us from when? Edwardian times, perhaps, from his clothing, but possibly before that. Was he a member of the families who had once lived here?

We retrieved him from the attic and hung him where he would not have too much sun, but could look at the house in which we presume he had once lived. He has revealed nothing more to us of his life and times, but continues to look at us in his soulful way—although perhaps a bit happier in having joined the life of the house once more. He gives no hint of his secrets, as he hangs in his new space, but remains our mystery, attic painting.

Cellar Bounty

W hen we arrived in this house, one of the few places relatively untouched was the cellar. Here we discovered higgledy-piggledy shelves, full of jars of produce. My husband reckoned some of them were from the era of the second world war, when planting and preserving (as in the "Victory Gardens") were advocated. The jars themselves were, in many cases, from that time.

Most likely the contents of those jars, yet sealed, would have been good, but, with a doctor-husband and my own, lay-person's knowledge of bacteria, it was decided not to be tasting any of the contents! Instead, everything was emptied into the garden—this was before we had begun our compost heap. We carried out jar upon jar and emptied each onto the earth. For the most part the smells were wonderful—and not only to us!

Soon we were surrounded by bees, wasps, flies of all kinds, who were less picky about trying these old preserves. They flew in and indulged. We were amazed. So happy were they with this unexpected bounty that we were able to stroke bees and butterflies without disturbing them. They were tamed. So ecstatic with this manna that we were not recognized as a potential danger. The broken social line between Man's dominion and Nature's was forgotten. For a few hours we were accepted as fellow earth-dwellers, instead of the threat we are usually considered to be. It was an amazing and memorable experience.

Windows

*A*lways, when visiting a house, particularly an old house, it is oft-times the windows that hold my interest. They are the eyes of the house, but seem to me to reflect the eyes, too, of bygone occupants.

As one passes through a room, it is fascinating to go to a window and look out on the view from that perspective. Much of course is changed—landscaping, either through destruction, or simply through growth. Early plantings are grown to maturity, thus changing the outlook. Fashions in gardening also change, thus so may have the view from the window. However, the position of the window, has, most often, not changed. To wander to a window is to follow in the footsteps of many others. The view may be altered, but the window is most likely the same. As are most of our human feelings. Men and women will have looked through these apertures in all moods, in all seasons, at all times of day and night.

Some will have looked out in joy, some in sorrow. Tears may have marked the glass and blurred the view. Some may have waved goodbye and others excitedly awaited an arrival. There will have been bright, summer days, with birds and flowers to see from this place as well as cold, winter days of uniformly grey aspect.

There will have been eyes and hearts full of hopes and those in despair, gazing from this very spot.

No doubt all of our emotions have been enacted while looking out of windows. They reflect both the inside and outside of our lives, in all their many diversities.

Always consider the windows. They could relate a great deal.

An Old House

*T*o many "modern" people we live a primitive life. Our older house has heat only downstairs and air-conditioning nowhere. The house, being built before the time of air-conditioning and central heat, has fireplaces and windows instead.

After a winter of frost on the insides of the windows and trying valiantly to keep fires stoked enough to keep us warm, we put in heat—downstairs. Upstairs we have big, fluffy, down bedding, hot-water-bottles—and a few cats!

As friends tell us "Throw another cat on the bed" when it is to be very cold! We open windows in good weather, armed against insects by "screens." These windows are well-placed to catch breezes and allow a flow of through-air. Situated on a hill, there are more breezes than would be imagined at lower levels— even on the hottest day.

Life with many cats does not preclude mice—even if lore tells us differently! They may not survive long, but they are there, sharing our home. We also entertain ants at certain times of the year, and, sometimes, a wasp's nest has managed to develop between window and screen. In some ways we are open to the workings of Nature and, as with many things, not all is perfect.

However, the open windows allow us to hear bird-song, the rustle of leaves and feel the welcome breezes even as we sit in a comfortable sofa, or lie in bed at night. It allows we "moderns" to remain a little in touch with our natural world.

Garden Creatures

*I*t has been impressed upon us how very diverse is our "wildlife." When we came here we worried that there were no birds—not a good sign. However, we soon realized why—there was no habitat for them.

We set about our gardening with a view to creating privacy and a place of solace and beauty for ourselves. At the same time realizing that what we loved and enjoyed was also a shared desire of our bird and animal friends. After many years of plantings, rearranging, loss, change, more rearranging, we now have a wonderfully private retreat, with diverse plantings of trees, shrubs, flowers, fruits and vegetables—and a wide range of visitors!

No longer do we worry that there are no birds. There are large numbers of birds, in all seasons. Some we class as "residents" who seem to be here all year. Feeding, nesting, raising babies—all right here in the garden. Others come and go, but we like to think they remember our garden and try to return, as we humans do with a favoured holiday destination.

There are bats, bees, wasps, butterflies, dragonflies, mice, voles, frogs and our fish. The odd tortoise has wandered through, possums, raccoons, cats (some we don't know!) and humming-bird moths. There are also many insects, a garden-snake has been seen and also birds of many varieties. All the birds we could wish for.

This makes us very happy.

Rain

We have had rain! Over the last few days, enough to show almost four inches on our rain gauge. The pool is full, the pond is full, the birdbaths are full, the water barrel is full. Every plant, even those under bigger trees and shrubs, is surrounded by wet soil and is standing up to its full height, filled with water!

The sky, having disgorged the weight of water from its over-laden clouds, is clear. The just-washed, clean-as-new blue, seen after storms. Clouds remain around, but are now pristine-white and fluffy, drifting along on the delicate, after-storm breeze, not one of them looking as if it was even distantly related to those who visited yesterday.

Rain has been needed and we have been lucky to receive only what could be used, without adding those amounts that cause problems. It has always been our policy to be careful for what is asked. Specifics are necessary. Simply asking for rain is not good.

That is when a year's supply comes down in a day, causing havoc, dismay and, oft-times, disaster. We always ask for a light, soaking rain, without wind, to fall preferably between midnight and six in the morning. This request allows as much as possible to be absorbed by those who need it before the sun tries to suck it all out ! She is a thirsty being and will take up all moisture available.

Sometimes our desires are granted—as of last night, when the perfect rain fell during the dark hours, before the sun was aware of what had happened.

Dead Fish and Bird

*T*his week, near the ending of August, has seen us find two dead fish and a dead bird in our pond. Found on a bright, sunny day makes it seem all the sadder somehow. The bird, a young sparrow, had drowned, maybe just too inexperienced to dip and sip. The fish, too, would suggest something untoward, yet they appear untouched by anything but death. They floated, gold as ever, only with their eyes glazed over and in the unnatural, unmoving poses of death. They were together—some kind of fishy suicide pact? It will remain unknown to we humans. We only know they died "under mysterious circumstances" and that we are sorry and sad. Three funerals in one day is too much!

A week or so on from the above incident, while feeding the fish, a darting was noticed in amongst the pond plants. Then they were seen—at least two baby fishes. Teeny, wee things, but already golden and enjoying life and all it holds. There and gone, as their game continued. Swift, adept, totally at home in their watery world. Ready to begin anew, where our two departed left off. It was a perfect example of "the cycle of life."

Of the on-going hopes of each species, of the exuberance of life, be it short, or long. There are many sparrows in the garden, some no doubt saddened by their loss, but going on with living, as all species must do as best they can.

Clean Air and "Earl"

*T*he outer, wide bands of "Earl" came on Friday, bringing not only gusts, but some rain, too. Bigger winds are quite rare here, so it was interesting to see the effects on the trees and shrubs as they bent and bowed until the gust was over.

The rain was very welcome after another prolonged dry spell. However, the most interesting and beautiful part of "Earl's" passing was the cleansing of the air. Saturday morning dawned as fresh and new as if it was the first ever. Leaves and needles shone and sparkled in a sunlight undimmed by a haze of humidity. Everything outlined against the purest, blue sky and wisps of whitest clouds. Even plants, who earlier had been showing signs of tiredness after blooming all summer in exceedingly hot, dry weather, assumed a new radiance, a depth of colour in their remaining blooms.

There also came a drop in temperature. Not such as to cause dismay, but enough to let us know, like the wild geese, that "beneath warm feathers, something cautioned frost." Dogs and cats are finding warmer snuggle places, birds appear to be eating more at the feeders. There are signs that a warning has gone out.

To be sure, our hot days are not yet over, but the clear air, free of humidity, reminds us that the season is changing. It is not yet quite fully an Autumn air. It is a gift of September and "Earl," giving Nature notice to be prepared. Enjoy the beauty, but hear the whisper of the next season's approach.

The Autumn Leaf

*A*n early September morning. A clear, blue sky. Feathery clouds and a jet trail. And, on the ground, the first Autumn leaf. A maple, still with some green, but mostly a mottled orange and yellow. There are no holes in it, no blemishes at all. It has fallen from its perch in a perfectly pristine condition. To lie on the yet-green of the grass, beside the blues and purples of asters, the reflourishing butterfly bushes, the berries of nandina. It signals to them all that their days in the sun and warm are becoming fewer. That this year's growth is about to end.

The trees for the most part remain green, but the passing has begun. Today one leaf, tomorrow another. Two, three and then a deluge of coloured rain falling to earth.

Soon what has been shaded will be open to the sun's rays and to moonlight. Rain will have no difficulty in finding its way to the ground. The rustle of wind in leafy branches will give way to open sighs as it finds its way through now-exposed wood.

Trees take on their slim, pared-down look, wearing the darker colours of winter and showing the simplest, most elegant shapes. They are ready now to flaunt their new streamlined looks against starkly-blue winter skies. To allow moonlight to turn them to silver. To play with the moon and stars in their tallest branches. To sparkle with frost and cover themselves in a blanket of snow. To rest and hope for renewal next spring.

Dragonflies

*D*ragonflies are special creatures. They have that type of metamorphosis that speaks to us of more than we may understand, but hope and wish does truly exist.

A dragonfly darting by, carefully following its route of surveillance, means menace to mosquitos and other less-desired sharers of our planet. My father, so badly affected by biting insects, considered the dragonflies amongst his best friends, to be cherished and admired!

We have the smaller damsel flies up to the heavy-duty, no-nonsense dragonflies. Each a wonder in its own way. A very stiff-looking body, supported by such light, gossamer wings. These very wings a kaleidoscope of colour. Veritable Tiffany creations in all their delicate beauty.

Dutiful in their patrols; back, forward, darting this way and that when necessary. Harbingers of death to some, a joyful chance to relax to another.

Resting momentarily on a leaf allows a closer look at these marvels. Perfectly balanced, powerful, yet so delicate to our human eye. They live their lives sharing our world, yet completely separate to most of us. Unseen by many of us, as they live their span, doing what their lives demand of them. A part of this wondrous earth we call home. Another link in the amazing chain. Every link adding something to the whole.

To those who dislike mosquitos, the dragonfly is an essential link.

Natural Wonders

A week of natural wonders!

Heavy rains, watering, filling, nourishing in the late afternoon, then the return of the sun for a last " hurrah" before bed. With the combination of wet and sun, a beautiful rainbow. The perfect arc across the sky, bypassing clouds and blue to show its palette of colour briefly before fading into nothingness once more.

A couple of mornings later, during the early breakfast period, a flock of geese going on their way. Quite low over the garden and honking "Good Morning" as their formation passed. They knew where they wished to go, keeping exactly on course until no longer visible to these somewhat bleary early-morning eyes.

Last night, a clear, early-evening sky promised the moon and stars later. And, true enough, before the complete darkness, a bright orange, perfect circle appeared over the hills. Bigger than usual it seemed as she slowly wandered up the sky until perched on top of a pine tree, looking like some bright Christmas-tree-topper.

As the journey continued, the orange paled until the more usual, wonderful silvery-white replaced that first burst of warmth.

Soon stars joined the display in the sky and in the garden the fireflies danced.

When sleep came, the moon had walked quite a bit of the night in her "silver shoon," giving a gentle, silent sheen to all she touched.

A Full, Harvest Moon

*T*oday has been hot for late September, and yet there is something in the air of Autumn. A smell on the breeze; a sense of tiredness in plants. A visual sense, too, in the seed heads formed, ready for another year's growth. The gatherings of birds about to fly off to other climes. A feeling that life is slowing down, readying for hibernation. Gathering seeds and food supplies and gradually battening down the hatches in readiness for whatever the winter months have in store. A sense of quiet preparation going on, almost invisibly, but with a definite purpose and determination.

Then tonight a full moon. Exquisite in its shape and colour. Not the pale, silvery moon of most nights, but tonight the first of what we call the "harvest" moons. These are tinged with a pale yellow-cum-orange and give a much warmer glow to the night sky. There is, of course, the scientific explanation— air particles, etc.—and while accepting this, we prefer to believe that the moon knows the season and occasion and dresses accordingly. She wears the colours of the wheat, safely harvested. She mimics, in a paler version, the pumpkins; the shades the leaves will show a short time from now.

She reflects the quiet calmness of a season which knows from long experience that it encapsulates death and plans for rebirth.

Sadness and happiness. The sense of a job well-done in the stores of the fruit, vegetables and grains.

A contentment and a hope.

The Chair

$\mathcal{A}$t about 8:30 am, nearing the end of July, providing it is a bright and sunny morning, the sun spotlights an old bent-willow chair in the garden. This may not sound in any way remarkable to many, but to me it has traces of the magical.

I am a child of our modern world, so am perfectly aware of the scientific explanations for this. My brain knows it can be explained in equations and formulae, but my heart and spirit say "Magic."

Magic, because the old chair is transformed. It takes on a new life. It glows. The places where the bark has worn away, shine as if newly polished.

It sits with its back to a maple tree, flanked now, too, by an errant cedar, quietly waiting for those few days in July when it becomes a star each sunny morning.

Waits patiently, while the sun finds the path through the myriad branches and leaves of several layers of trees and shrubs.

It seems unworried. Sits quietly as always—and then it is 8:30 am! The path through the branches and leaves has been found and the chair is centre-stage!

It is not demonstrative about being thus chosen each sunny day, but if you know the chair well, you see the change.

There is an inner glow, a warmth, even something of a smile. All very reserved and dignified, as an old chair should be. One that has seen many weathers, known the perch of birds, the falling of leaves—and being able to bask in sunshine at 8:30 am on late July mornings.

Baby Birds

*T*here seem to have been many baby birds born this year—and survived. Fewer egg shells found broken on the ground. Fewer dead, featherless babies to bury. Thus, nearing this end of July, there are many first-seasoners at the feeders.

They are particularly noticeable in that they look so much healthier than their poor worn-to-a frazzle parents.

Although bright, fully feathered, ready to go and face their new lives, many still arrive with a parent—chancing their luck at being fed, pathetically fluttering their wings at their sides. As with most children, they are spoiled and, often as not, the parent will pop a few morsels into the ever-hungry mouth.

It is also fascinating to see that, as with the young of all species, they can be gauche and clumsy. Not quite judging the landing correctly, nearly falling from a branch as they preen. Balance has to be learned.

Something not needing to be learned, something ingrained in their genetic coding is being on the "lookout" at all times. Not when eating. Not when drinking. Not when bathing, is the guard down. Yet some are still caught—by cats, by birds of prey. Obviously, like us all, there are times when they are not alert enough to hidden dangers and some pay dearly for that lapse.

This year, though, it would seem that the living and thriving have outnumbered the less fortunate.

Humming Birds

*F*or the first time we know we have more than one humming bird in the garden!

Normally, at this bee-balm-time, we see "a" humming bird, or two, or three—but never more than one at a time.

This year we have seen two together and another close by, so we know we have had at least three visiting us.

They are fascinating, but exhausting to watch. I can feel my arms begin to sag watching the beating of their wings, the colours of their wee bodies shimmering in the sun as they sup on the nectar they love.

Looking at a butterfly bush yesterday, I was amazed all over again at the popularity of this plant. Every sort of butterfly, bee, the humming bird moth—and the humming bird itself all enjoying themselves.

This was an entrancing moment. To watch the moth and the one with whom it shares a name enjoying "lunch" together at the same "restaurant."

It occurred to me, too, that there was no conflict amongst all the differing, winged creatures there. They were too busy collecting, supping, enjoying the bounty of this lovely bush. If one flitted into another, they simply separated and went to another bloom, realizing there was enough for everyone.

It was relaxing to watch, so quietly was it all done. All the fluttering and flitting and supping—no sounds to bother the ear. Just the busy-ness of the wings giving the sense of work being involved in the venture.

Rain

*R*ains have come this evening, after a very hot, very dry day.

A day when any movement caused clothes to stick, the brow to dampen.

Then in late afternoon the clouds changed. The fluffy blobs began to grow and join together with their neighbours. Next, the colour changed from bright white to grey, to darker grey.

As the wind rose, we heard a boom in the distance and soon after, the rain, gentle at first, then pounding on the roofs and paths.

A collective sigh was heard all over the garden by plants, shrubs, trees and creatures—including those two-leggeds who water when there is no rain!

There is a relaxation in knowing that X amount of rain has fallen, allowing a breathing space before the next vigil of the skies begins.

A respite for a few days before signs of distress return to those anchored in the ground, unable to pack-up and leave for parts less stressful to their survival. It brings to mind Milton's words—"They also serve who only stand and wait." The trees and shrubs who serve us by their beauty and shade-giving ; the flowers which droop in the mid-day sun, but revitalize in the cooler evening to display their beauty another day; the grasses that tell us of even the slightest breeze—all standing and waiting, in all weathers, to serve us with their blessings, despite hardships, extremes and sometimes torture, over which they have no control.

Dusting

*a*s always, when dusting and cleaning, a closer bond is made with our "things" and although they are just that, because they are ours they are part of the family. They live with us. See us happy and sad. Help to entertain our guests. Rest peacefully at night and await us when we have been away.

Each piece has its own story, some longer than their life with us. However, most of this is secret and we can only be sure of the history since coming to our home.

Every item is precious to us. Not because of any monetary value, but because it was chosen by us, or for us, with love and hopes of pleasure in its ownership. This piece was found when we visited this town, or this particular area ; this one is from so-and-so; this was given for a birthday, Christmas, anniversary.

Some are much older than others. Some are showing age, with cracks and chips and twistings, but all remain beautiful to us—maybe more so because of the character they show, the marks of a long life. The fact that they have survived through many years, many homes, many owners.

The younger ones, even the new ones, settle in together with the more venerable like a multi-generational family, each bringing its own beauty to the whole, its own special spirit to the rooms of our home and a joy to this person's dusting experience!

The Porch

*O*ur screened porch is a haven for all who share our home—not least our-selves. It has proven itself worthy of the time and effort it took to design, build and paint. Now settled-in on the back of the house, as if it had always been there.

It began life as a porch only, but quite soon after added the designation of "screened" and this is what has made it the wonderful haven it has become. Not only does it keep out weather, but it works hard—and has an almost 100% record—at keeping out those creatures and insects we prefer to live without.

There is something of the secretive and magical in being able to sit out-side, untouched by biting, stinging, annoying insects. They may be our fellow earthlings, and it is so wonderful that they may be that—but on the other side of the screen! We do not wish to kill them, we just don't want to have them know us on the personal basis most of them seem to desire.

To sit at any time, during sun, rain, wind, hot, cold, is fascinating. We are as in a "hide," invisible to birds and squirrels in daytime, raccoons and pos-sums at night.

We are able to watch the sun set out for its day, as it rises over the trees and sends into us the only rays that reach inside in summer, keeping it cooler and welcoming on hot days. After sunset, as we sit in our wee haven, we see the glow of the day fade to dark, etching the trees against the sky. The bats flap overhead, dipping into the pool for a drink. Fireflies emerge to light the darkness.

With Nature, but on our terms. It is a good plan.

Fireflies

$\mathcal{S}$ometimes the magical is hard to see and sometimes it is quite obvious. Nature hides many of her magical items, so that only the true lookers and believers will see them. However, for those of a less studious bent, there are wonders more easily seen.

Fireflies are of this group, all that is required is a darkish area and eyes ready to witness these flashes in the dark.

Beginning at ground level and rising with each glow, they ascend to the tops of the trees. Magical. Now here, now gone, little beams of light. They are all the more amazing for their silence. In our noisy world it is especially wonderful to find quiet things, going about their business, beautifully and without fanfare. It has to be wondered how we humans would fare if at birth we were equipped with only a small lamp with which to find our way to love and life. A silent communication of flashing lights, like ships across an ocean.

We do use light in our lives, but so much of it is associated with noise : street lights, airport-runway lights, shop lights. The light itself is not noisy, but until we see the fireflies on a dark night, reaching for the silent stars, or a quietly, but brightly lit moon-filled night sky, we forget. Light is a quiet thing; we have made it appear noisy by our use of it. To the fireflies and other night creatures, to the moon vines and daturas the quietness of starlight and moonlight is enough.

The Train

When living in the centre of a village, or town, it has to be accepted that there will be some noise. Having chosen to live in this place, there is no point in expecting the silence of a bare hillside. Some noises are more than could be wished, but these are rare and must be tolerated for their duration.

In our wee village there are trains—running right through the middle of it—not a river, but trains. They travel from east-to-west and west-to-east—but not at the same time. There is only one track. There are, however, several road crossings, so every train must make itself known by blowing its horn as each is approached. The sound is more muted at first, becoming a crescendo as the crossing is reached. Once over the crossing the sound becomes more muted again and we are left with the sound of the rolling stock as it tries to keep up with the engine. Some of said stock are poorly oiled, squeaking and screaming as they are pulled, unwillingly it would seem, from A-to-B. Now mostly containers, the only changing characteristics are the colours and names on the sides and the sprayings of graffiti on most. Fascinating legends of import/export and of idling in yards somewhere long enough to be "signed" by the artists.

Some of the trains must employ several engines to pull the heavy, long loads. This is especially true for those traveling west-to-east. In this direction there is an incline which causes many an engine to wish it had taken better care of its boilers when it was younger.

But best of all. If you are near the track and wave, still today, as often as not, the driver will wave back !

Night

Last night was a night of several things, noticed mainly because it was a night of not sleeping. There was no moon, but there were stars, with the "Plough"—known as the Big Dipper here—clearly visible. Someone said they couldn't live anywhere they couldn't grow corn, so it would be hard for me to live where the Plough could not be seen. It has been with me all my life, a friend of long-standing, in good times and in bad.

It was also noted how often the garden lights went from their muted "at rest" glow to their bright beam of "something's here."

Sometimes it's the branches in the wind, but last night it was a raccoon, one of the several creatures we call "our resident—whatever."

This beautiful, big person was alone on this occasion, so all was quietly done and would have been invisible but for the light.

Then there was the twitting of a bird. Unusual in the dark hours. It didn't sound distressed and was probably, like myself, restless, alert and wondering how long it was until it was time to begin a new day.

The frogs completed the night's observations. Along with the crickets, they sang until dawn. There appeared to be three of them taking part, each with his/her own distinctive voice. The smallest sound was the soprano, a slightly stronger alto and the louder, deep tones of a base. To my wide-awake ears they seemed to sing in turn, each adding their few notes, in order of pitch, before pausing and repeating. It is presumed this constituted some wonderfully popular tune in the frog world!

Sparrow and Datura

A very small sparrow, possibly a baby, has come to the feeder this early morning and has sat down completely in amongst the seed. It has its wee head looking out to the world and is munching, while resting. He/she is so enjoying this leisurely, early breakfast and refuses to budge, even when bigger birds arrive. Maybe this is the bird heard in the sleepless night, no doubt feeling tired and wishing for some sleep now. Or perhaps he/she partied with the frogs—not wisely, but too well!

One of the daturas, a wonderful dusk-to-dawn bloomer, has six perfectly-formed trumpets still open this morning. They look like the brass section of a band, grouped together as they are. Their proximity to the pond and the frogs makes me wonder if they were playing at last night's event, silent only to my poor, human ears. Fortunately, they are visible to the human eye and their stark, cool whiteness is radiant on this hot, August morning. From seed-pod—so unlike what would be imagined if only the flower was known—to elegantly, elongated bud, with the perfect folds, to full-blown trumpet-flower, this is a highly interesting, quietly exotic plant. No wonder Georgia O'Keefe painted it.

Needing little to no care, but preferring to be left alone to perform where and when it chooses, this is a much-enjoyed addition to our late-summer garden. Anticipated, watched in all its fascinating stages of development. Admired for its simple elegance and creamy perfume.

www.ingramcontent.com/pod-product-compliance
Lightning Source LLC
Chambersburg PA
CBHW022135280326
41933CB00007B/709